STRUM IT GUITAR

AUTHENTIC CHORDS
ORIGINAL KEYS
COMPLETE SONGS

THE VERY BEST OF ERIC CLAPTON

Cover photo by Adrian Boot / London Features International, LTD

ISBN 0-634-05374-4

HAL•LEONARD®
CORPORATION

7777 W. BLUEMOUND RD. P.O. BOX 13819 MILWAUKEE, WI 53213

Visit Hal Leonard Online at
www.halleonard.com

CONTENTS

Bad Love

Words and Music by Eric Clapton and Mick Jones

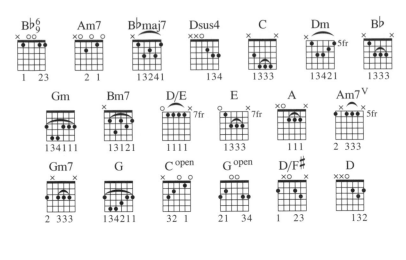

Intro
Freely

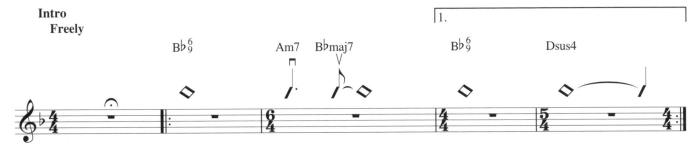

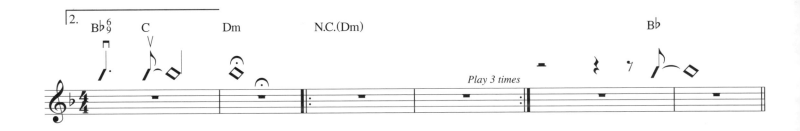

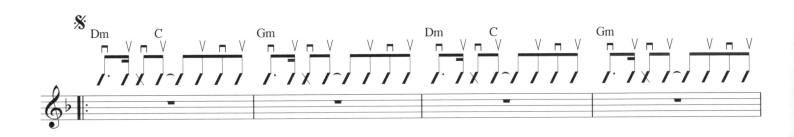

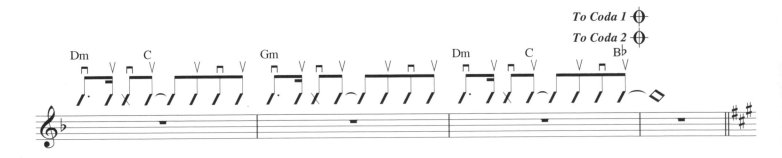

Verse

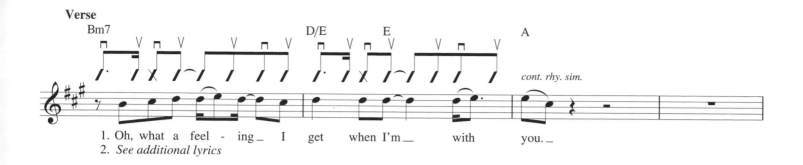

1. Oh, what a feel - ing __ I get when I'm __ with you. __
2. *See additional lyrics*

You take my heart __ in - to ev - 'ry - thing __ you __ do, __ and __ it
See additional lyrics

Pre-Chorus

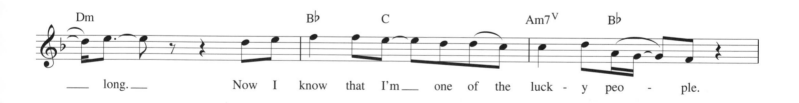

makes me sad __ for the lone - ly peo - ple, I walked that road for __ so __

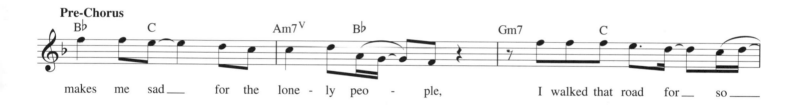

__ long. __ Now I know that I'm __ one of the luck - y peo - ple.

Chorus

Your love is mak - ing me __ strong. __ I've had e - nough of bad

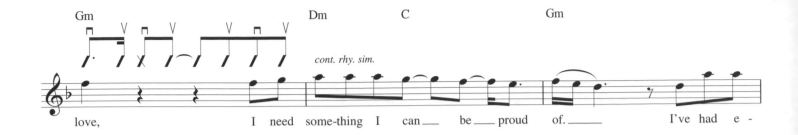

love,   I need some-thing I can__ be __ proud of. _____ I've had e -

2nd time, D.S. al Coda 1

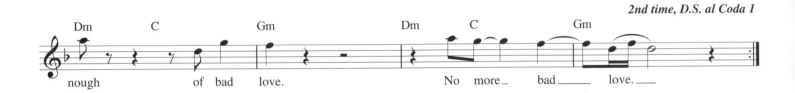

nough   of bad love.   No more_ bad _____ love. ____

⊕ Coda 1

Interlude   **Guitar Solo**

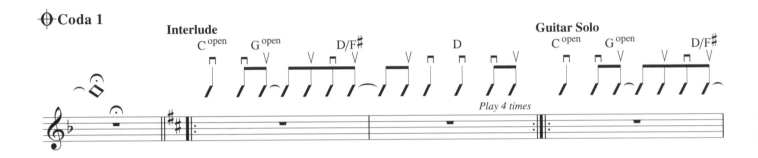

Play 4 times

⊕ Coda 2

8th time, D.S. al Coda 2   **Outro-Chorus**
w/ Voc. ad lib. on repeats

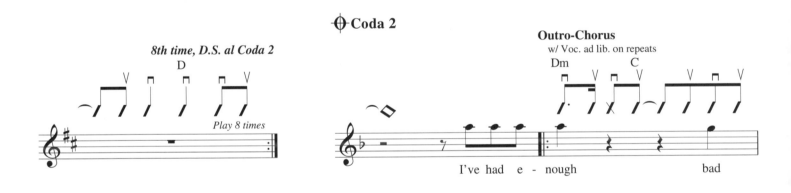

Play 8 times

I've had e - nough   bad

Repeat and fade

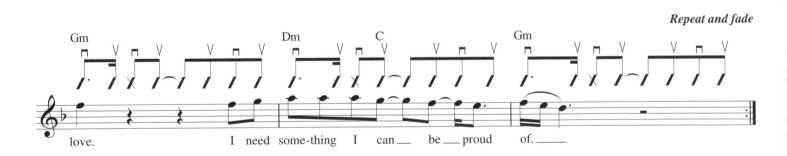

love.   I need some-thing I can__ be __ proud of. _____

Additional Lyrics

2. And now I see that my life has been so blue
With all the heartaches I had 'til I met you.

Pre-Chorus But I'm glad to say now that's all behind me
With you here by my side,
And there's no more memories to remind me.
Your love will keep me alive.

For Your Love

Words and Music by Graham Gouldman

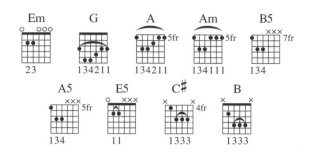

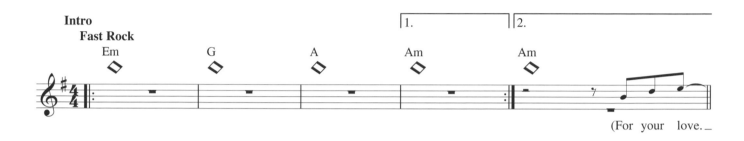

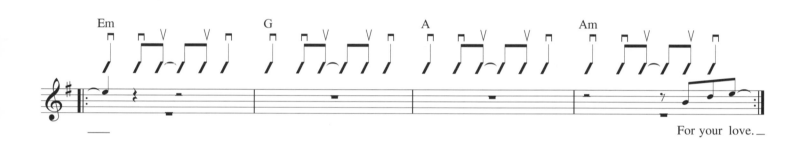

(For your love.

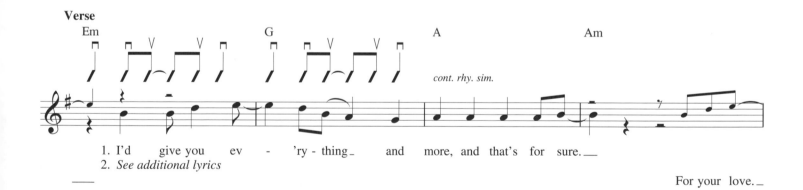

For your love.

Verse

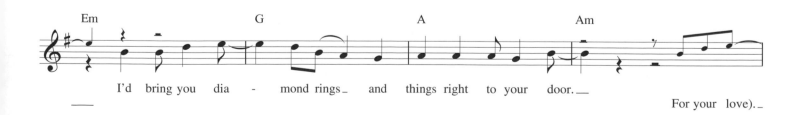

1. I'd give you ev-'ry-thing and more, and that's for sure.
2. *See additional lyrics*

For your love.

I'd bring you dia-mond rings and things right to your door.

For your love).

To thrill you with __ de - light, __ I'd give you dia - monds bright. __

To Coda ⊕

There'll be days I will __ ex - cite __ to make you dream of __ me __

Chorus

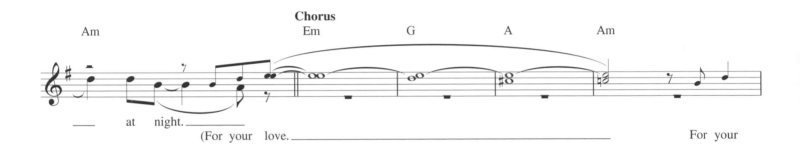

__ at night. __ (For your love. _____ For your

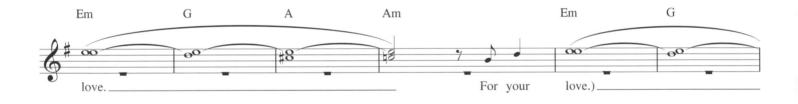

love. _____ For your love.) __

Slower
N.C.

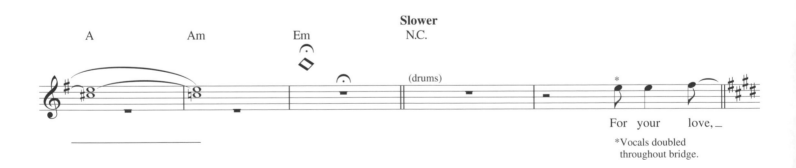

(drums)

For your love, __

*Vocals doubled throughout bridge.

Bridge

B5   A5

__ for your love, ____ I would give the __ stars __ a - bove. __

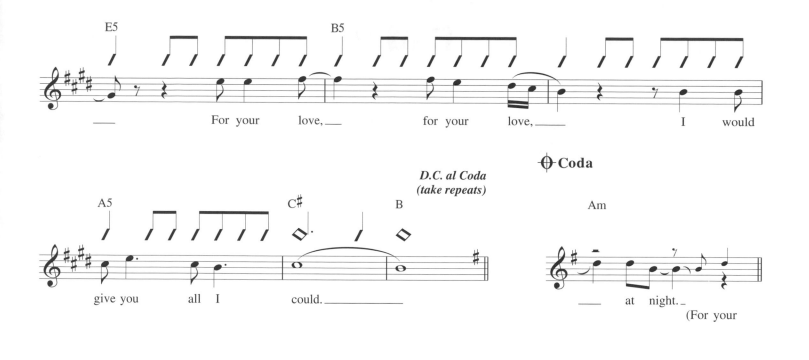

D.C. al Coda
(take repeats)

⊕ **Coda**

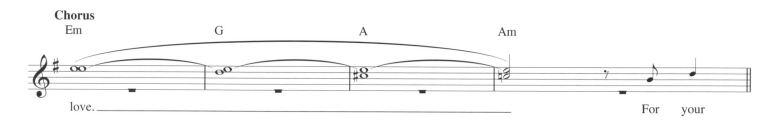

Chorus

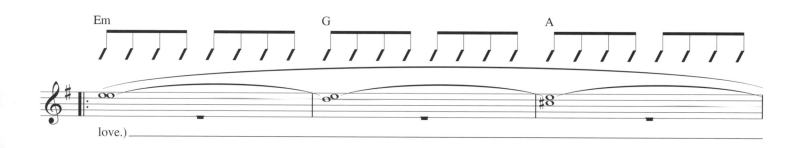

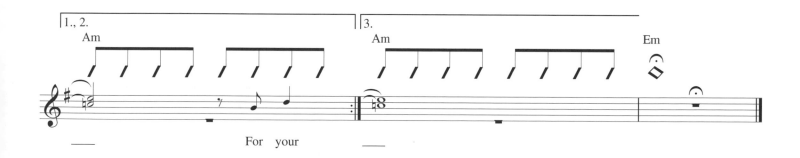

Additional Lyrics

2. I'd give the moon if it were mine to give.
   (For your love.)
   I'd give the stars and the sun before I'd live.
   (For your love.)
   To thrill you with delight,
   I'd give you diamonds bright.
   There'll be days I will excite
   To make you dream of me at night.

Badge

Words and Music by Eric Clapton and George Harrison

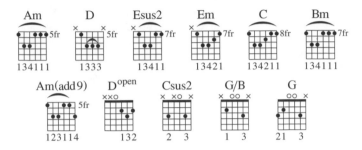

1. Think-in' 'bout the
2. *See additional lyrics*

times you drove__ in my car.__

Think-in' that I might have drove__ you too far.__

And I'm think-in' 'bout the love that you made on my ta - ble.

Yes, I told__

Additional Lyrics

2. I told you not to wander 'round in the dark.
I told you 'bout the swans, that they live in the park.
Then I told you 'bout our kid, now he's married to Mable.

Bell Bottom Blues

Words and Music by Eric Clapton

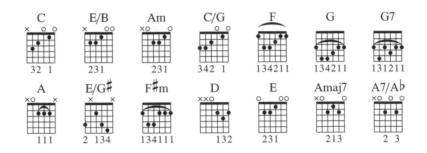

Intro
Slow Ballad

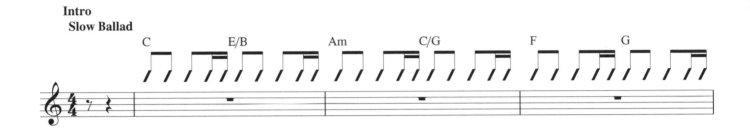

Verse

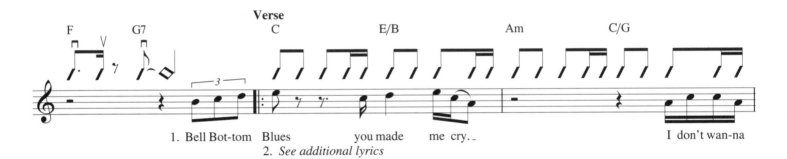

1. Bell Bot-tom Blues   you made   me cry._
2. *See additional lyrics*

I don't wan-na

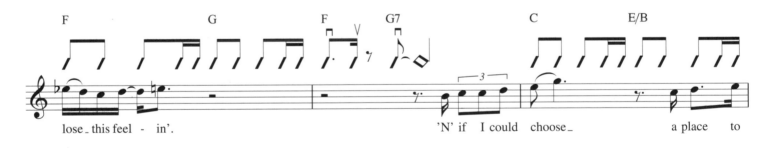

lose _ this feel - in'.   'N' if I could   choose _   a place to

die,   it would be   in _____ your _ arms. _

Pre-Chorus

Do you wan-na see me crawl a - cross the floor to you?

Do you wan-na hear me beg you to take me back? I'd glad - ly do it be-cause

Chorus

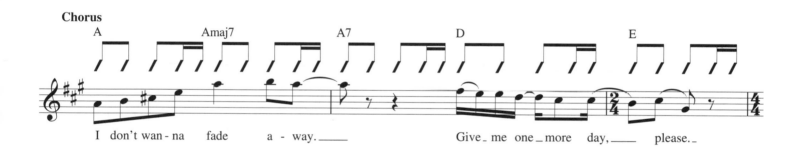

I don't wan-na fade a - way. Give me one more day, please.

To Coda

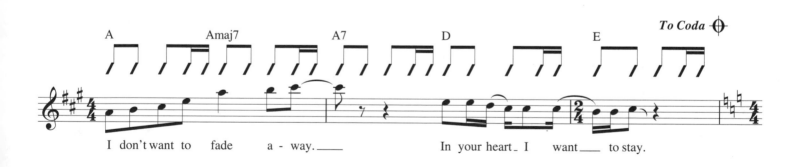

I don't want to fade a - way. In your heart I want to stay.

Guitar Solo

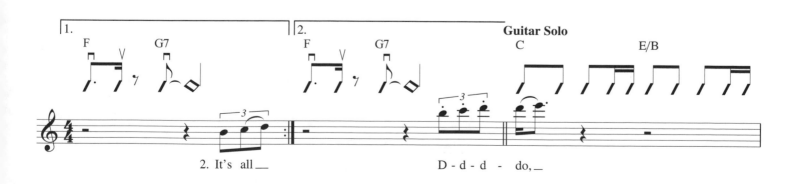

1.

2. It's all

2.

D - d - d - do,

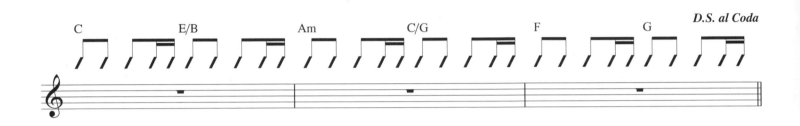

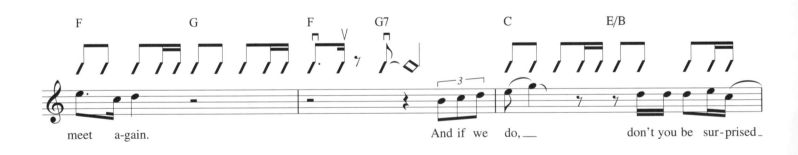

3. Bell Bot-tom Blues, don't say, __ "Good-bye." We're sure-ly gon-na

meet a-gain. And if we do, __ don't you be sur-prised __

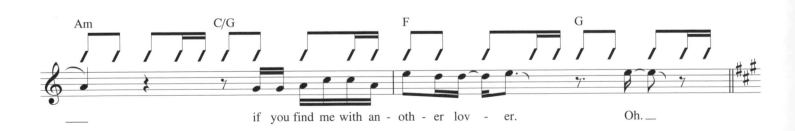

__ if you find me with an-oth-er lov - er. Oh. __

Pre-Chorus

Do you wan-na see me crawl a - cross_ the floor_____ to you?

Do you wan-na hear me beg you to take me back?_____ I'd glad - ly do it be-cause

Outro-Chorus

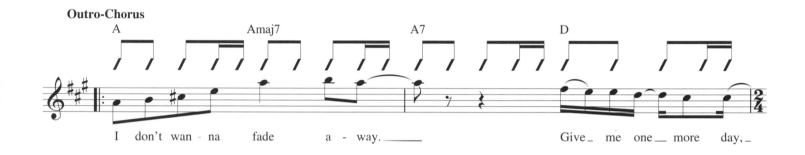

I don't wan - na fade a - way._____ Give_ me one_ more day,_

_____ please._ I don't want to fade a - way._____

_____ In your heart_ I want_ to stay.

Additional Lyrics

2. It's all wrong, but it's alright.
The way that you treat me, baby. Mm.
Once I was strong, but I lost the fight;
You won't find a better loser.

Change the World

featured on the Motion Picture Soundtrack PHENOMENON

Words and Music by Wayne Kirkpatrick, Gordon Kennedy and Tommy Sims

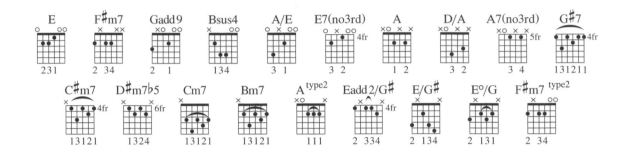

Intro

Moderately

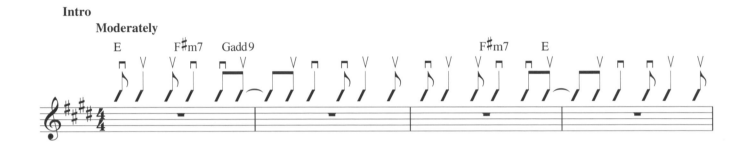

Verse

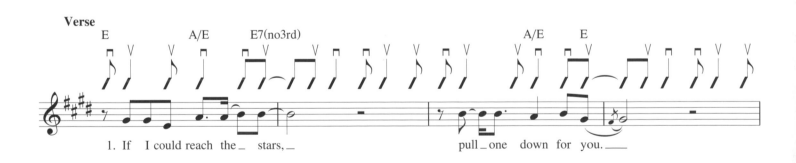

1. If I could reach the stars, pull one down for you.

Shine it on my heart so you could see the truth.

Then this love I have in - side   is ev - 'ry-thing it   seems.

But for now I find   it's on - ly in my dreams.   And I can

Chorus

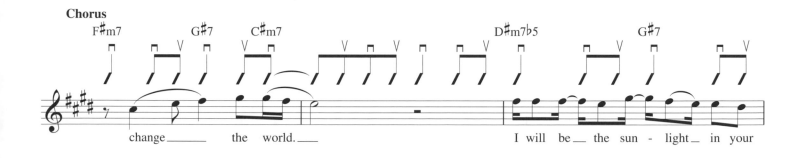

change   the world.   I will be the sun - light in your

u - ni - verse.   You would think my love was real - ly   some - thing good, ba - by,

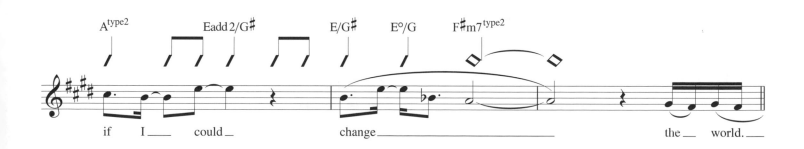

if I   could   change   the world.

Interlude

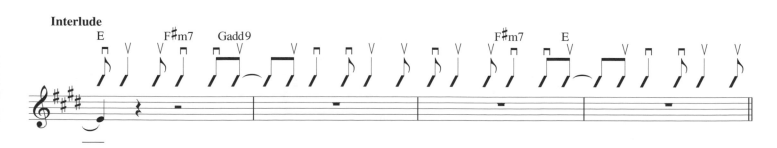

Verse

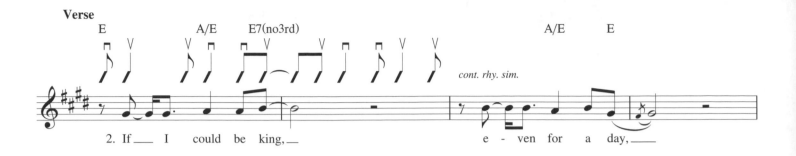

2. If __ I could be king, __ e - ven for a day, __

I'd take you as my __ queen, __ I'd have it no oth - er way. __

And __ our love would rule __ in __ this king - dom we have __ made. __

Till then I'd be a __ fool, __ wish - ing for the day. __ And I can

Chorus

change __ the world. __ I will be __ the sun - light __ in your u - ni-verse. __

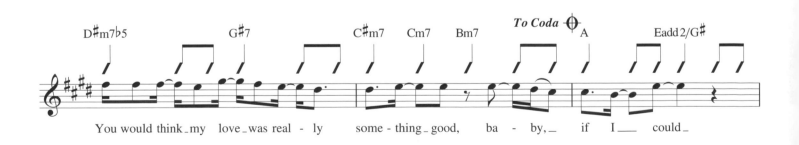

You would think __ my love __ was real - ly some - thing __ good, ba - by, __ if I __ could __

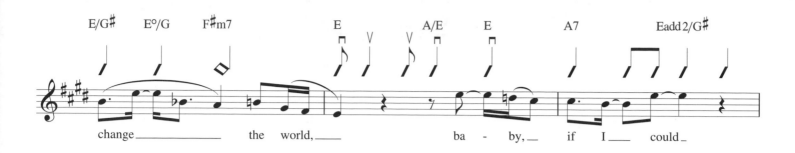

change _____ the world, _____ ba - by, __ if I ___ could_

change _____ the _ world. ___

Guitar Solo

cont. rhy. sim.

I can

D.S. al Coda

Coda

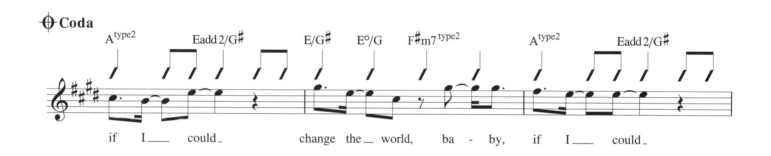

if I ___ could_ change the _ world, ba - by, if I ___ could_

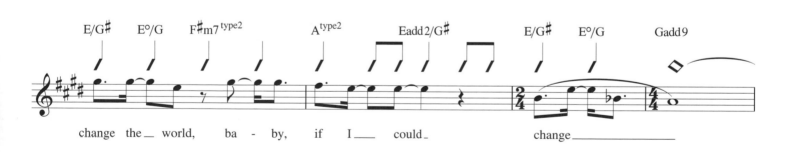

change the _ world, ba - by, if I ___ could_ change _____

Outro

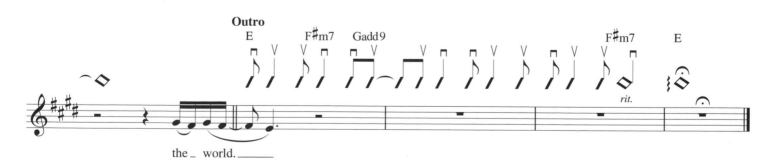

the _ world. _____

rit.

Cocaine

Words and Music by J.J. Cale

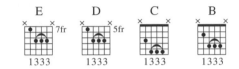

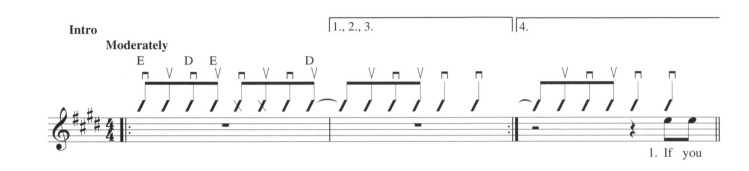

1. If you wan-na hang out, you've got-ta take her out, co-caine.

2., 3. *See additional lyrics*

If you wan-na get down, down on the ground, co-caine.

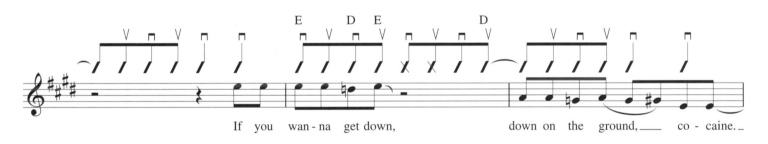

She don't lie, she don't lie, she don't lie,

co-caine.

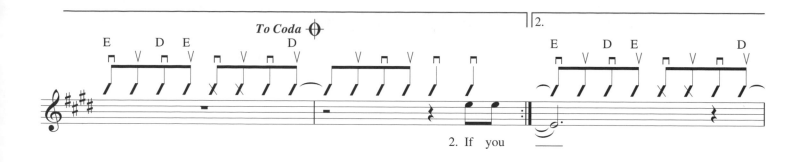

2. If you

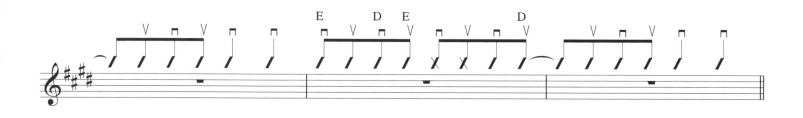

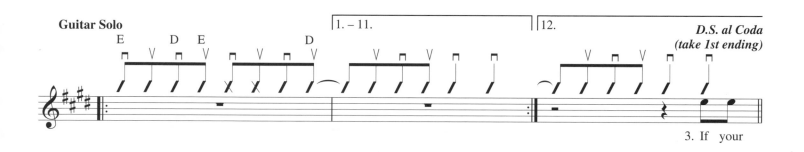

Guitar Solo

3. If your

She don't lie, _____ she don't lie, _____ she don't lie, _____ co - caine. __

Outro-Guitar Solo

Repeat and fade

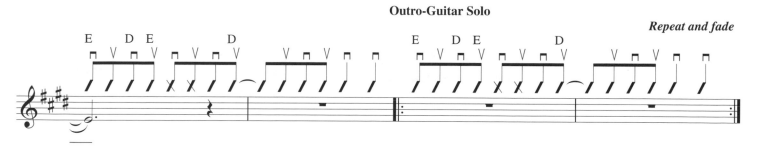

Additional Lyrics

2. If you got bad news, you wanna kick the blues, cocaine.
   When your day is done an' you wanna run, cocaine.
   She don't lie, she don't lie, she don't lie,
   Cocaine.

3. If your thing is gone and ya wanna ride on, cocaine.
   Don't forget this fact, can't get it back, cocaine.
   She don't lie, she don't lie, she don't lie,
   Cocaine.

Comin' Home

Words and Music by Eric Clapton and Bonnie Bramlett

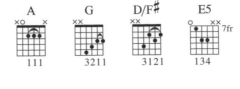

Intro
Moderately

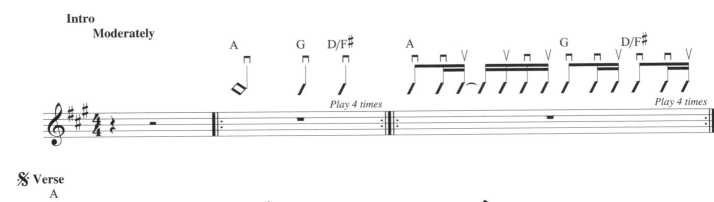

Verse

1. Been out __ on the road _____ 'bout six months too long. I want you so __

2. *See additional lyrics*

__ bad, _____ I can __ hard - ly stand __ it. I'm so __ tired __

__ and I'm all __ a - lone. _____ We'll __ soon __ be to -

To Coda

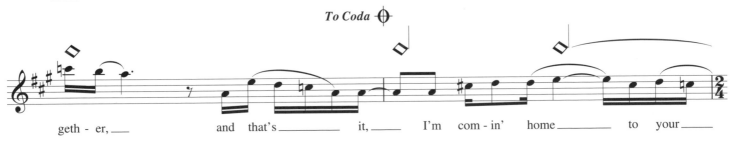

geth - er, __ and that's _____ it, __ I'm com - in' home _____ to your __

Interlude

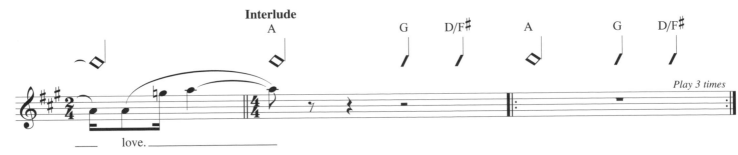

__ love. _____

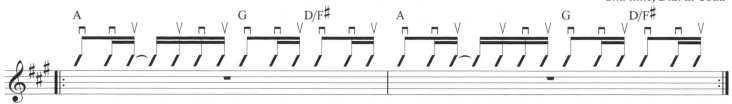

⊕ **Coda**

Guitar Solo
E5

Play 5 times

why I'm com-in' home _____ to your _ love. _____

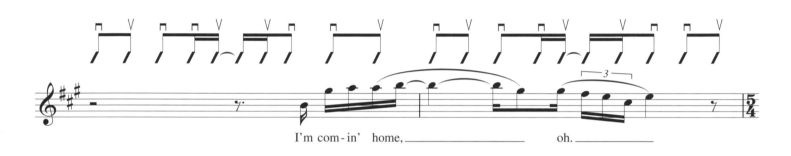

I'm com-in' home, _____ oh. _____

Interlude

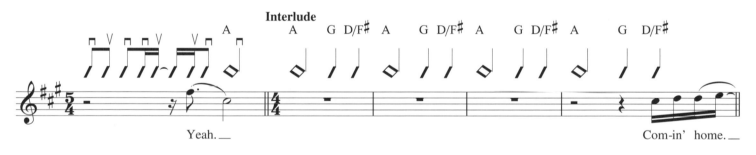

Yeah. ____   Com-in' home. ____

Outro
w/ Voc. ad lib. on repeats

Repeat and fade

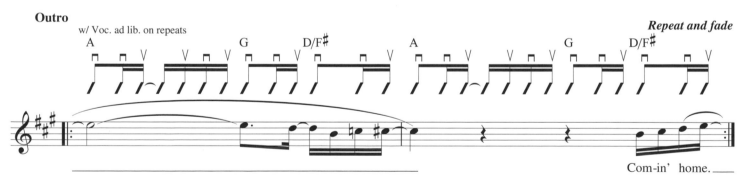

Com-in' home. ____

Additional Lyrics

2. Hitchhiking on the turnpike
   All day long.
   Nobody seems to notice,
   They just pass me on by.
   To keep from going crazy,
   I gotta sing my song.
   Got a whole lot of lovin',
   And baby that's why I'm comin' home to your love.

Hello Old Friend

Words and Music by Eric Clapton

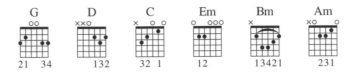

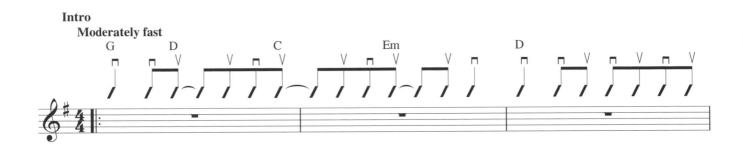

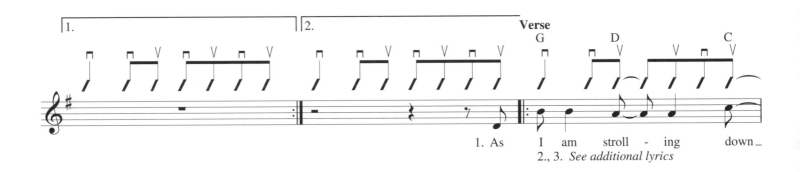

1. As I am stroll - ing down _

2., 3. *See additional lyrics*

_ the gar - den path, _

I

saw a flow - er glow - ing in _ the dark. _

It

looked so pret - ty and _ it was u - nique. _

I

had to bend down just to have a peek. Hel - lo old friend,

% Chorus

(Hel - lo old friend.) it's real - ly good to see

you once a - gain. Hel-lo old friend, it's real - ly good to see

(Hel - lo old friend.)

To Coda ⊕

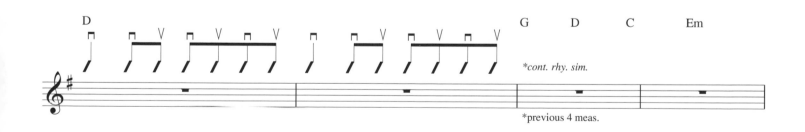

you once a - gain.

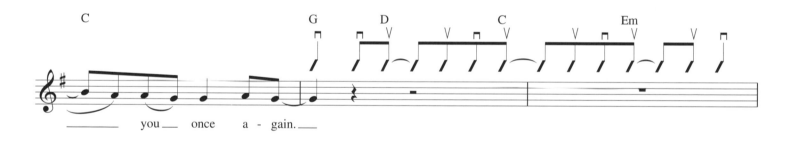

cont. rhy. sim.

previous 4 meas.

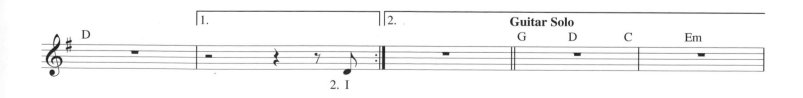

1. **2.** **Guitar Solo**

2. I

25

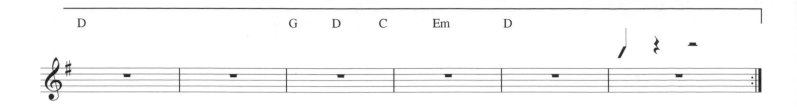

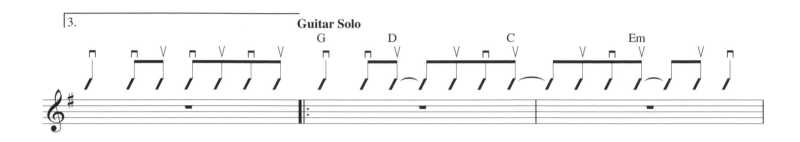

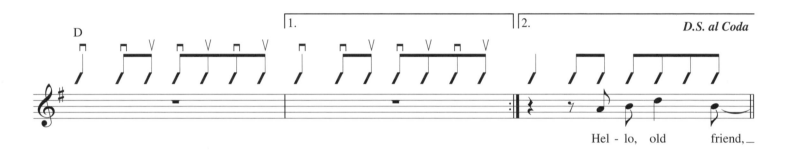

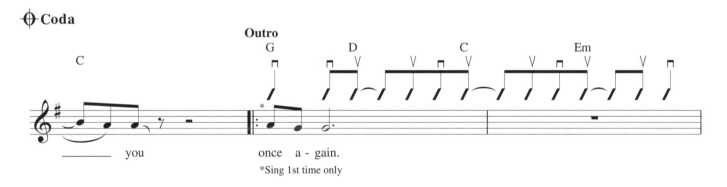

Hel - lo, old   friend, __

◆ Coda

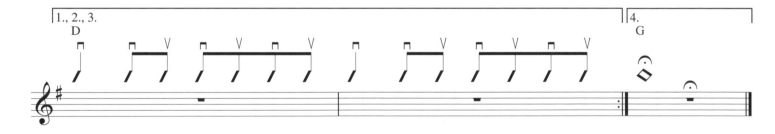

Outro

_____ you   once a - gain.

*Sing 1st time only

Additional Lyrics

2. I saw you walking underneath the stars.
   I couldn't stop 'cause I was in a car.
   I'm sure the distance wouldn't be too far
   If I got out and walked to where you are.

3. An old man passed me on the street today.
   I thought I knew him, but I couldn't say.
   I stopped to think if I could place his frame,
   But when he tipped his hat I knew his name.

I Shot the Sheriff

Words and Music by Bob Marley

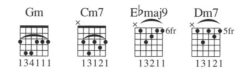

Chorus

I shot the sher - iff, but I swear it was in self-de-fense.

I shot the sher - iff,

{ and they say it is a cap - i - tal of - fense.

{ but I swear it was in self - de - fense.

Verse

3. Free-dom came my way one day, an' I start - ed out of town,

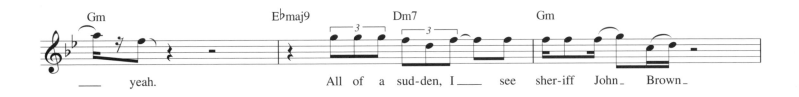

yeah. All of a sud-den, I see sher-iff John Brown

aim - in' to shoot me down, so I shot, I shot him

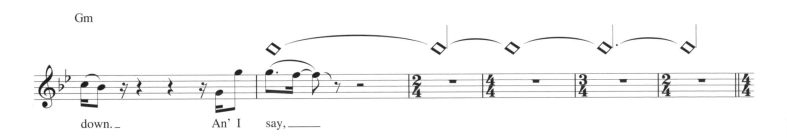

down. An' I say,

%. Chorus

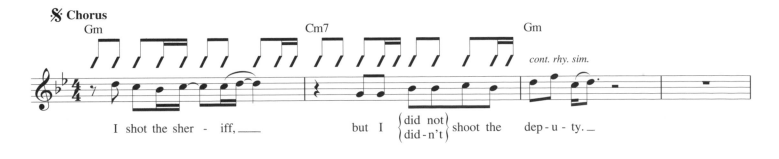

I shot the sher - iff, but I { did not } { did-n't } shoot the dep - u - ty.

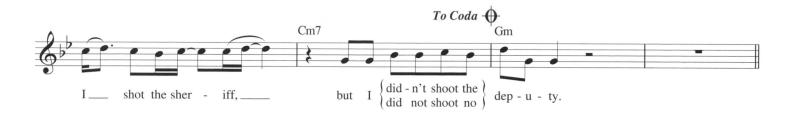

I ___ shot the sher - iff, ___ but I { did - n't shoot the / did not shoot no } dep - u - ty.

Verse

4. Re - flex - es got the bet - ter of me, ___ and what ___ is ___ to be,

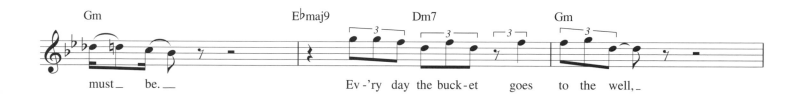

must ___ be. ___ Ev -'ry day the buck - et goes to the well, ___

but one day, the bot - tom ___ will ___ drop ___ out. ___ Yes, one day ___ the bot - tom will ___

___ drop out. ___ But I ___ say, _____

Coda

Outro *Repeat and fade*

dep - u - ty, ___ oh ___ no. ___

Additional Lyrics

2. Sheriff John Brown always hated me.
   For what I don't know.
   And ev'ry time that I plant a seed,
   He said, "Kill it before it grows."
   He said, "Kill it before it grows." I say,

I Can't Stand It

Words and Music by Eric Clapton

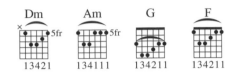

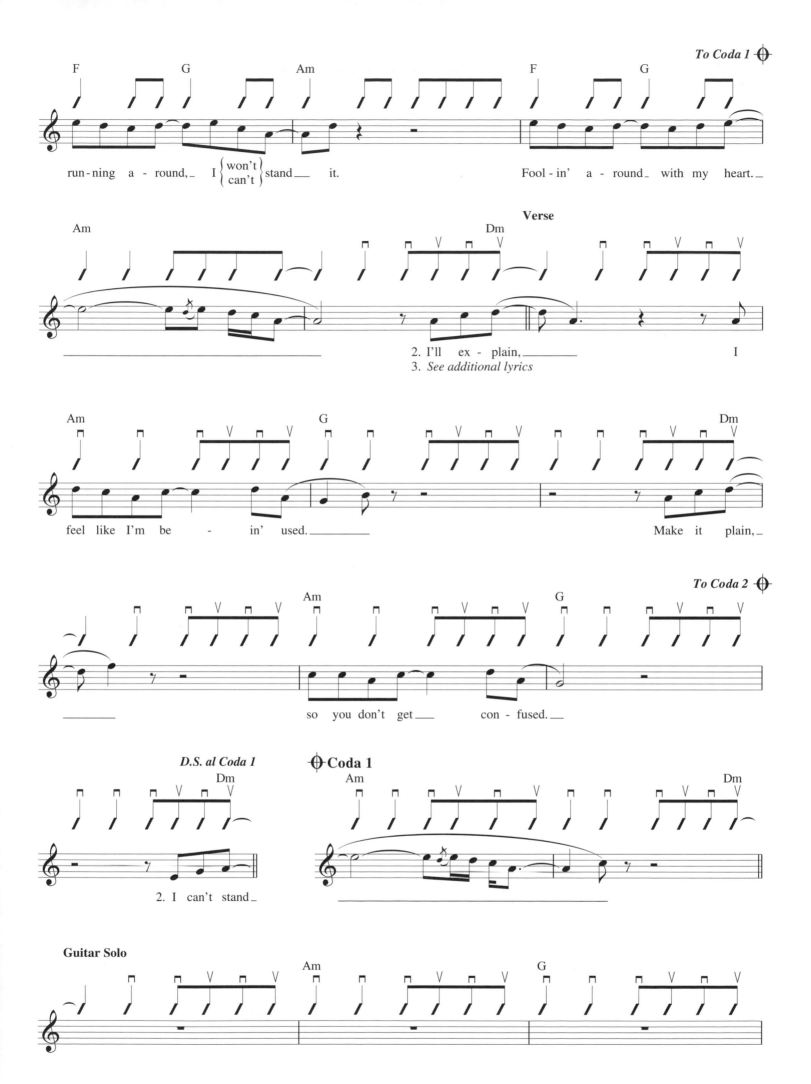

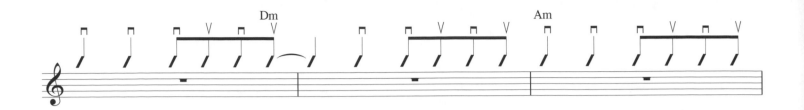

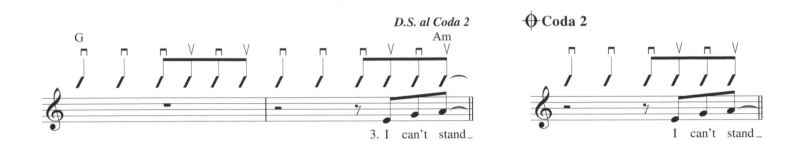

D.S. al Coda 2   ⊕ **Coda 2**

3. I can't stand_

I can't stand_

Chorus

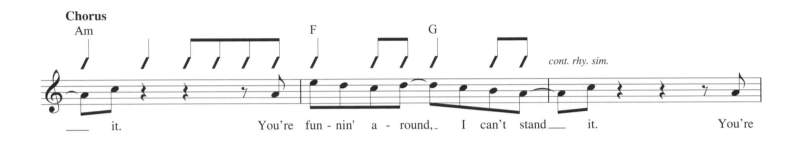

cont. rhy. sim.

_ it. You're fun - nin' a - round,_ I can't stand _ it. You're

play - in' a - round,_ I can't stand _ it. You're fool - in' a - round,_ I can't stand_

_ it. You're run - nin' a - round,_ I can't stand _ it. You're

play - ing a - round,_ I can't stand _ it. Fool - in' a - round,_ I can't stand_

_ it. Run - nin' a - round,_ I can't stand _ it.

Additional Lyrics

Chorus 3. I can't stand it.
You're running around, I can't stand it.
You're foolin' around, I can't stand it.
You're playin' around with my heart.

   3. It's time,
Time for me to let you know.
Ain't no crime,
No crime to let your feelings show.

Knockin' on Heaven's Door

Words and Music by Bob Dylan

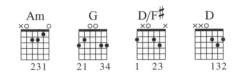

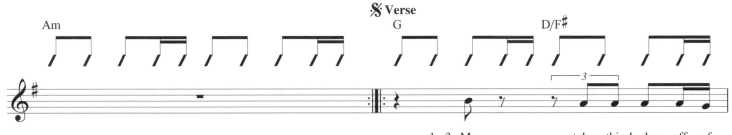

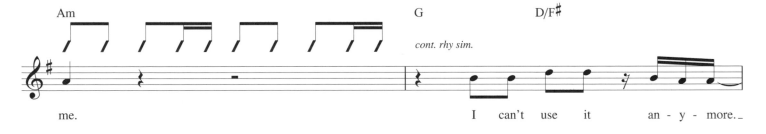

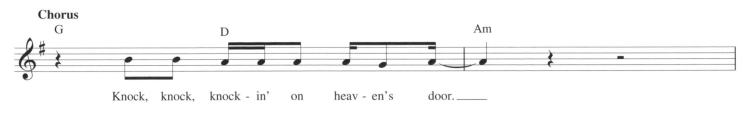

Additional Lyrics

2. Ma, take these guns away from me.
   I can't shoot them anymore.
   There's a long black cloud followin' me.
   Feel like I'm knockin' on heaven's door.

Lay Down Sally

Words and Music by Eric Clapton, Marcy Levy and George Terry

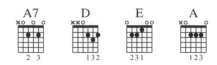

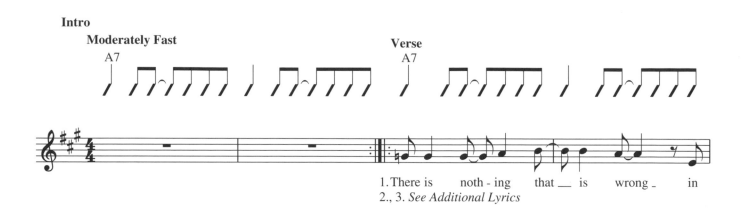

1. There is noth-ing that __ is wrong __ in
2., 3. *See Additional Lyrics*

want-ing you __ to stay __ here __ with me.   I

know you've got ___ some - where __ to go, __ but won't you make __ your - self __

___ at home __ and stay with me? __   And don't you ev - er leave. __

Lay down, Sal - ly, and rest you in __ my arms. __

Don't you think __ you want __ some - one __ to talk __ to? Lay down Sal -

- ly. No need to leave __ so soon. __ I've been try - ing all __

__ night long __ just to talk to you. __ 2. The

Additional Lyrics

2. The sun ain't nearly on the rise,
   And we still got the moon and stars above.
   Underneath the velvet skies,
   Love is all that matters;
   Won't you stay with me?
   And don't you ever leave.

3. I long to see the morning light
   Coloring your face so dreamily.
   So don't you go and say goodbye.
   You can lay your worries down
   And stay with me.
   And don't you ever leave.

Layla

Words and Music by Eric Clapton and Jim Gordon

beg - gin' dar - lin', please._ Lay - la, _____ dar - lin' won't you ease my wor - ried

mind?_

Verse

2. Tried to give you_ con - so -
3. *See additional lyrics*

la - tion, your old man had let you down._

Like_ a_____ fool, I fell in love_ with you. You turned my whole world up - side

𝄉 Chorus

down. Lay - la, _____ got me on my knees._ Lay - la, __

beg - gin' dar - lin', please. ___ Lay - la, _____

Additional Lyrics

2. Make the best of the situation,
   Before I fin'ly go insane.
   Please don't say we'll never find a way.
   Tell me all my love's in vain.

My Father's Eyes

Words and Music by Eric Clapton

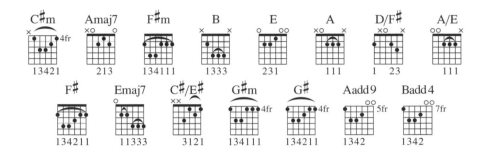

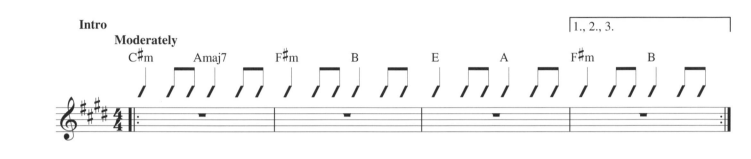

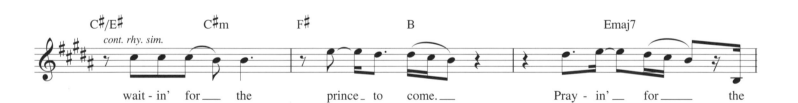

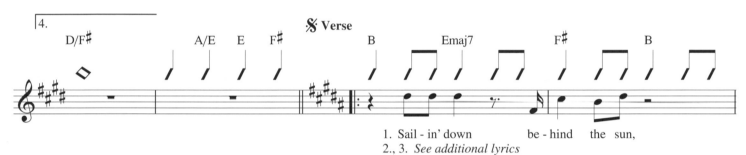

1. Sail - in' down   be - hind   the sun,
2., 3. *See additional lyrics*

wait - in' for ___ the   prince ___ to   come. ___   Pray - in' ___ for ___   the

heal - in' rain   to   re - store ___   my   soul   a - gain.

Pre-Chorus

1. Just   a   tour - ing,   on ___ the ___ run.   And how did   I   get here?
2., 3. *See additional lyrics*

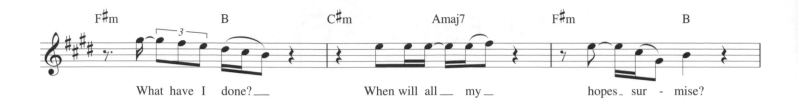

What have I done?___ When will all___ my___ hopes___ sur - mise?

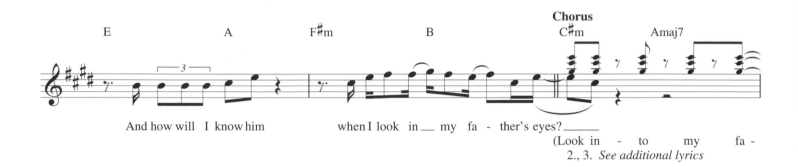

Chorus

And how will I know him when I look in___ my fa - ther's eyes?___
(Look in - to my fa-
2., 3. *See additional lyrics*

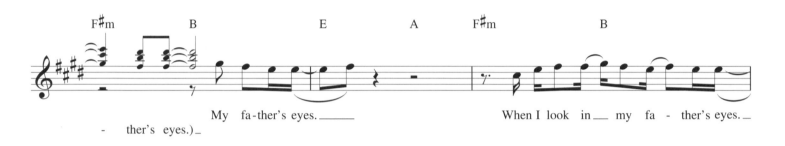

My fa-ther's eyes.___ When I look in___ my fa - ther's eyes.___
- ther's eyes.)___

To Coda ⊕

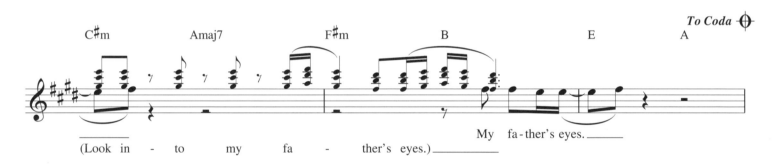

My fa-ther's eyes.___
(Look in - to my fa - ther's eyes.)___

Guitar Solo

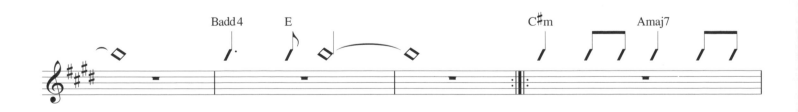

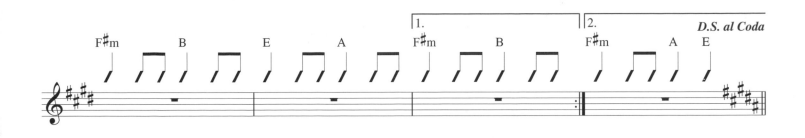

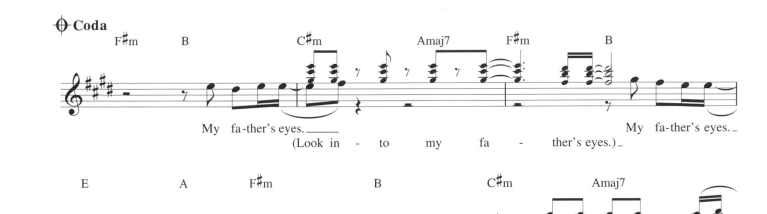

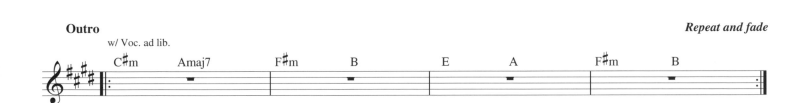

Outro

Repeat and fade

w/ Voc. ad lib.

Additional Lyrics

2. Then the light begins to shine.
   I hear those ancient lullabies.
   And as I watch the seedling grow,
   Feel my heart start to overflow.

3. Then the jagged edge appears
   Through the distant cloud of tears.
   I'm like a bridge that was washed away.
   My foundation's one made of clay.

Pre-Chorus 2. Where do I find the words to say?
   How do I teach him? What do we play?
   Bit by bit, I've realized
   That's when I need them.
   That's when I need my father's eyes.

Pre-Chorus 3. And as my soul slides down to die,
   How could I lose him? What did I try?
   Bit by bit, I've realized
   That he was here with me
   And I looked into my father's eyes.

Chorus 2. My father's eyes.
   That's when I need my father's eyes.
   My father's eyes.

Chorus 3. My father's eyes.
   I looked into my father's eyes.
   My father's eyes.
   My father's eyes.
   My father's eyes.
   I looked into my father's eyes.
   My father's eyes.

Let It Grow

Words and Music by Eric Clapton

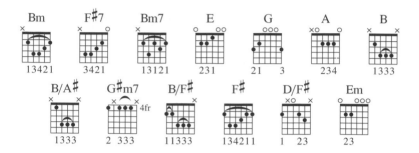

Verse
Moderately

1. Stand-ing at ___ the cross - roads, try'n' to read ___ the signs
2., 3. *See additional lyrics*

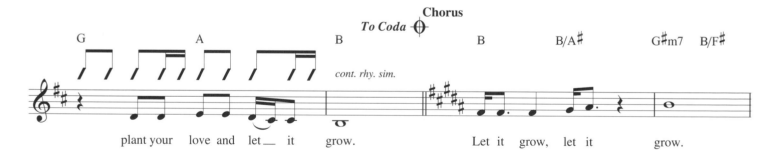

to tell me which way I should go to find ___ the an - swer, ___ and all the time ___ I ___ know,

Chorus

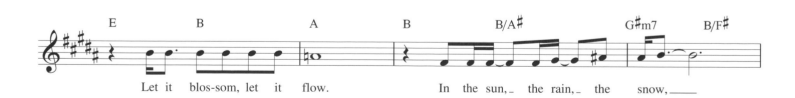

plant your love and let ___ it grow. Let it grow, let it grow.

Let it blos-som, let it flow. In the sun, ___ the rain, ___ the snow, ___

love is love-ly, ___ let ___ it grow. so let ___ it flow. ___

Additional Lyrics

2. Looking for a reason to check out on my mind.
   Trying hard to get a friend that I can count on,
   But there's nothing left to show.
   Plant your love and let it grow.

3. Time is getting shorter. There's much for you to do.
   Only ask, and you will get what you are needing.
   The rest is up to you.
   Plant your love and let it grow.

Running on Faith

Words and Music by Jerry Williams

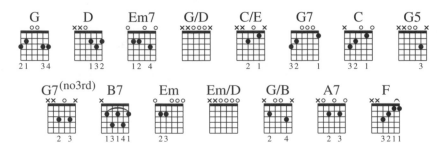

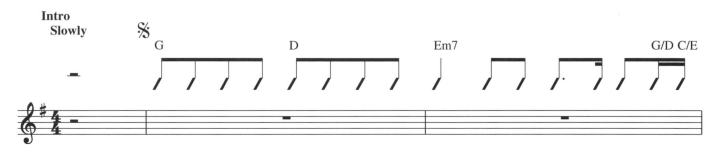

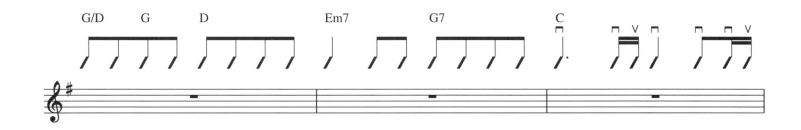

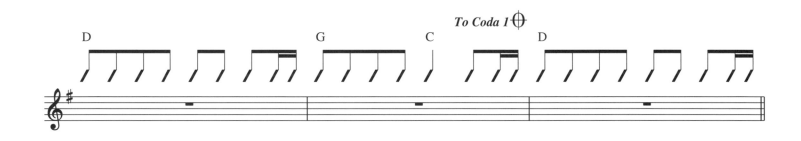

1. Late - ly I've been run - nin' on _____ faith. _____

What else _ can a poor _ boy _ do? _____ But my

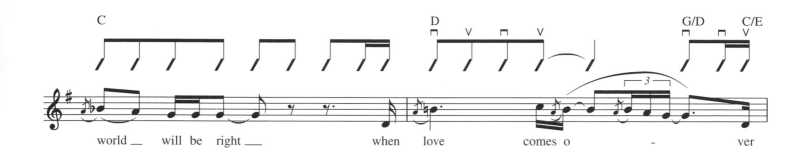

world _ will be right _ when love comes o - ver

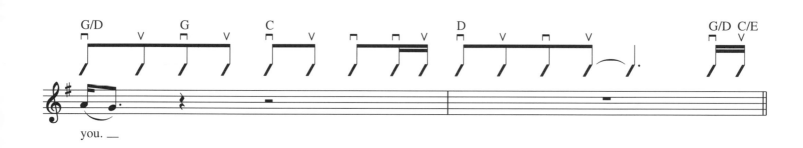

you. _

Verse

2. Late - ly I've been talk - in' in _____ my sleep.

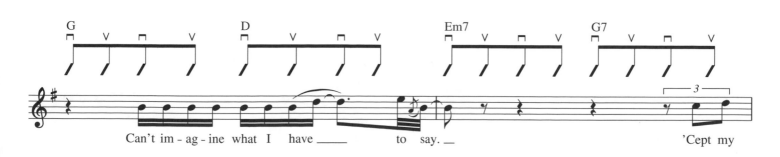

Can't im - ag - ine what I have _____ to say. _ 'Cept my

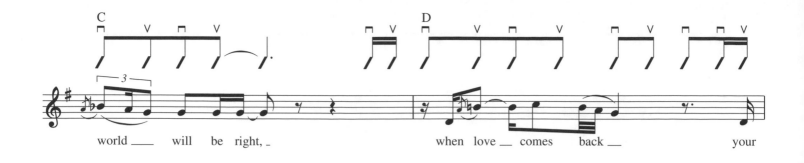

world ___ will be right, _ when love ___ comes back ___ your

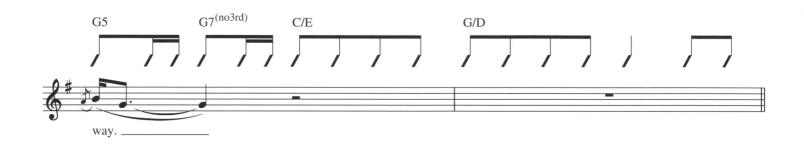

way. _____

Bridge

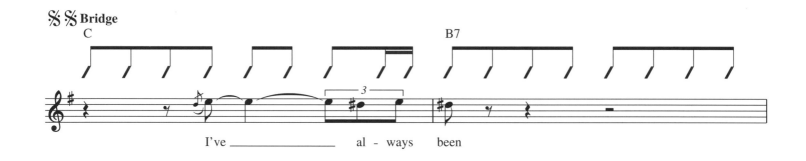

I've _____ al - ways been

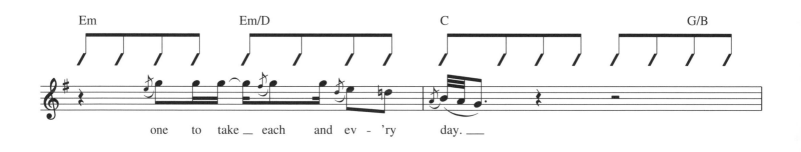

one to take ___ each and ev - 'ry day. ___

Seems ___ like 'bout ___ now _____ I'd find a love ___ who

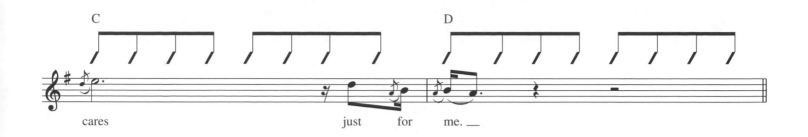

cares   just   for   me. __

Verse

3., 4. Then we'd go run-nin' on faith. __

All of our dreams   will come   true, _____   and our

To Coda 2

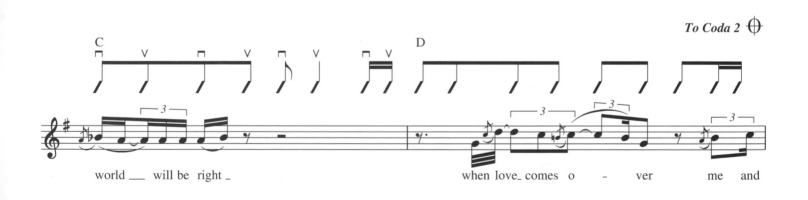

world __ will be right _   when love_ comes o - ver me and

D.S. al Coda 1

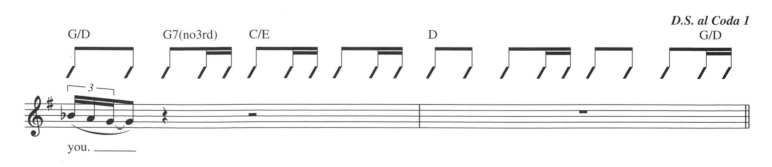

you. _____

Outro-Guitar Solo

love ___ comes o - ver you. ___

Said when love ___ comes o - ver you.

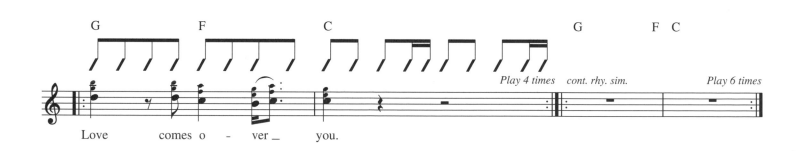

Love comes o - ver ___ you.

Rubato

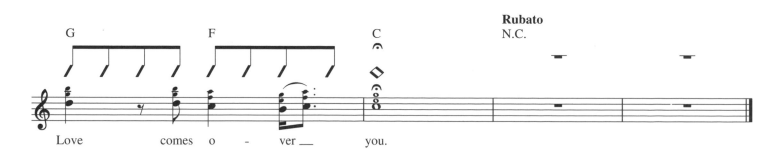

Love comes o - ver ___ you.

Superman Inside

Words and Music by Eric Clapton, Doyle Bramhall II and Susannah Melvoin

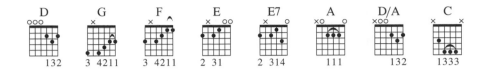

Drop D tuning:
(low to high) D–A–D–G–B–E

Intro
Moderately

𝄋 **Verse**

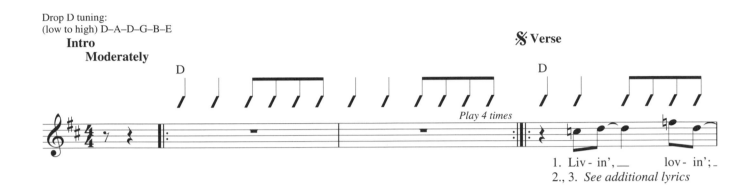

Play 4 times

1. Liv - in', lov - in';
2., 3. *See additional lyrics*

___ ain't gon - na waste my life ___ sing - in' ___ mu - sic. ___

___ Some days the sun don't shine. ___

Pre-Chorus

I don't wan - na be the one, ___ the one that can

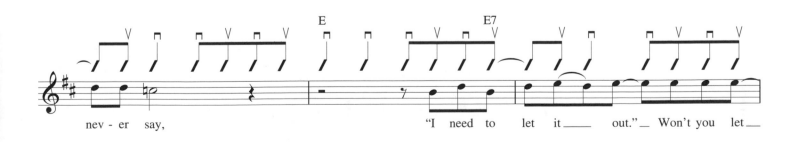

nev - er say, "I need to let it ___ out." Won't you let ___

Coda 1

Chorus

And look in the mir - ror. E - ven with a bro - ken heart I find... Keep on push - in'; get - ting clos - er to peace of mind. Look in the mir - ror.

E - ven with a bro - ken heart, I find liv - ing is so sweet.

To Coda 2

Now it's Su - per - man in - side.

Interlude

(Su - per - man in - side.

Su - per - man, Su - per - man in - side.)

D.S.S. al Coda 2

Coda 2

Outro
w/ Voc. ad lib. till fade

Repeat and fade

(Su - per - man, Su - per - man. Su - per - man in - side.)

Additional Lyrics

2. Give it all up, surrender thankfully.
   Fall down on my knees, my hands open wide.

3. No more runnin'; ain't gonna hide away.
   I'm standin' outside in the pouring rain.

White Room

Words and Music by Jack Bruce and Pete Brown

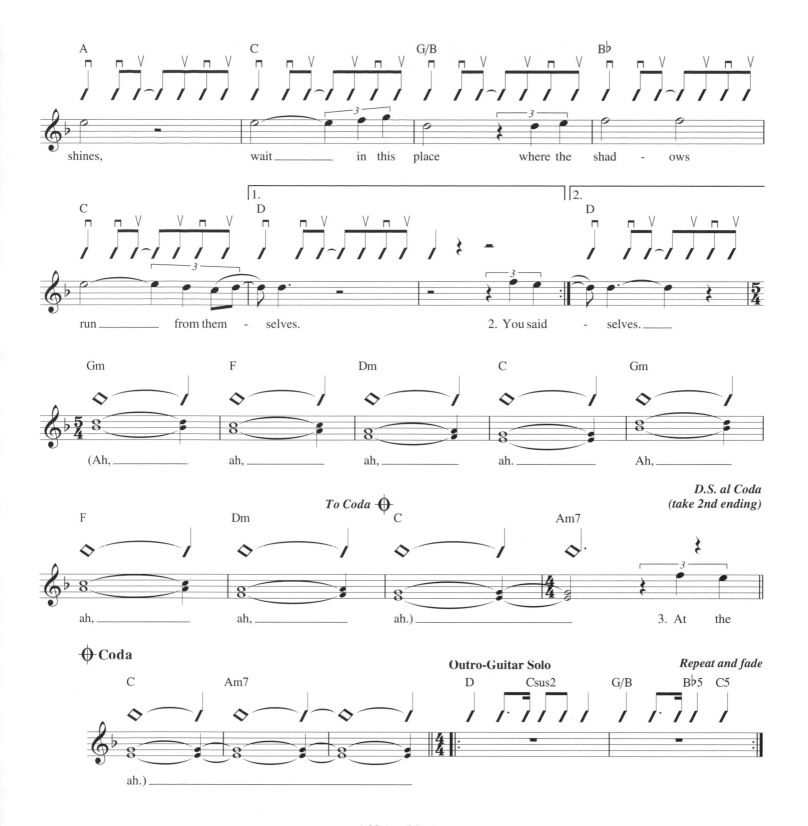

Additional Lyrics

2. You said no strings could secure you at the station.
Platform ticket, restless diesels, goodbye windows.
I walked into such a sad time at the station.
As I walked out, felt my own need just beginning.

Chorus 2. I'll wait in the queue when the trains come back,
Lie with you where the shadows run from themselves.

3. At the party, she was kindness in the hard crowd.
Consolation for the old wound now forgotten.
Yellow tigers crouched in jungles in the dark eyes.
She's just dressing, goodbye windows, tired starlings.

Chorus 3. I'll sleep in this place with the lonely crowd.
Lie in the dark where the shadows run from themselves.

Wonderful Tonight

Words and Music by Eric Clapton

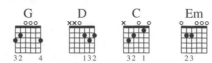

Intro
Moderately

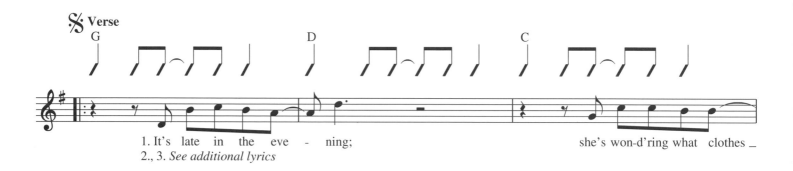

Verse

1. It's late in the eve - ning; she's won-d'ring what clothes __
2., 3. *See additional lyrics*

cont. rhy. sim.

__ to wear. __ She puts on her make - up

and brush-es her long __ blonde hair. __ And then she asks __

__ me, "Do I look all right?" __ And I say, "Yes, you look

To Coda ⊕ |1.

won - der - ful _____ to - night." __

I feel won - der - ful ___ be -

cause I see ___ the love ___ light in ___ your eyes. Then the won - der of it all ___

___ is that you just don't ___ re - al - ize ___ how much ___ I love ___

D.S. al Coda

___ you.

Coda

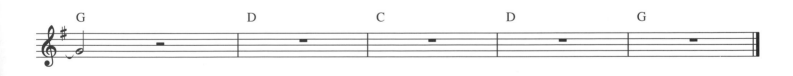

___ "Oh, my dar - ling, you are won - der - ful ___ to - night."___

G D C D G

___

Additional Lyrics

2. We go to a party, and ev'ryone turns to see
This beautiful lady that's walking around with me.
And then she asks me, "Do you feel alright?"
And I say, "Yes, I feel wonderful tonight."

3. It's time to go home now, and I've got an aching head.
So I give her the car keys and she helps me to bed.
And then I tell her, as I turn out the light,
I say, "My darling, you are wonderful tonight."

Tears in Heaven

Words and Music by Eric Clapton and Will Jennings

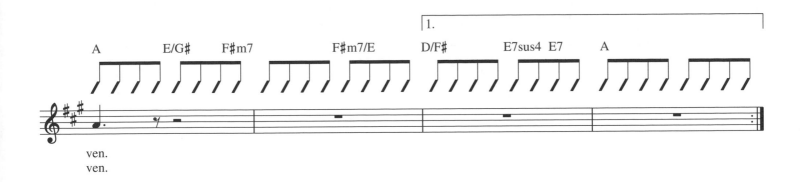

ven.
ven.

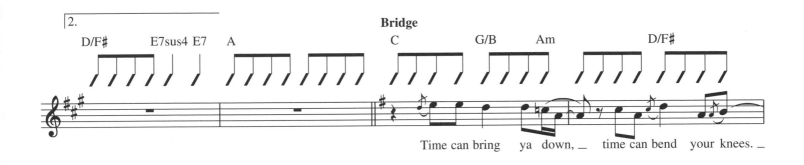

Time can bring ya down, ___ time can bend your knees. ___

Time can break your heart, ___ have ya beg - gin' please, ___

beg - gin' please. ___

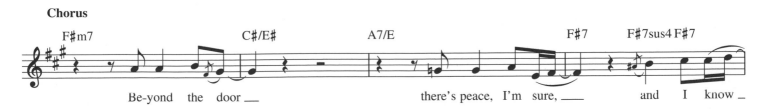

Be - yond the door ___ there's peace, I'm sure, ___ and I know ___

there'll be no more ___ tears _ in hea - ven.

D.S. al Coda

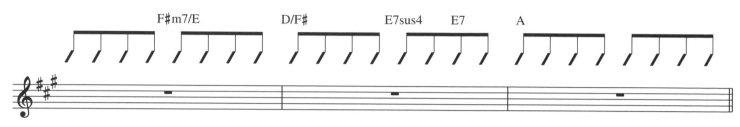

$\oplus$ **Coda**

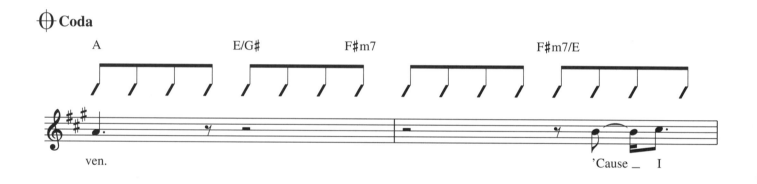

ven. 'Cause _ I

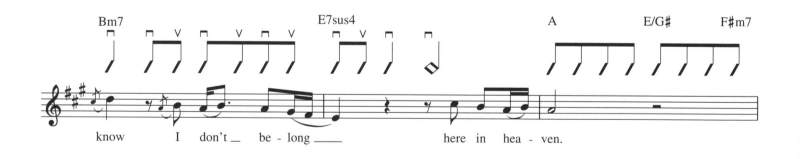

know I don't _ be - long ___ here in hea - ven.

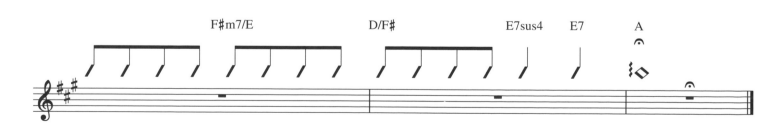

STRUM IT GUITAR LEGEND

Strum It is the series designed especially to get you playing (and singing!) along with your favorite songs. The idea is simple – the songs are arranged using their original keys in lead sheet format, providing you with the authentic chords for each song, beginning to end. Rhythm slashes are written above the staff. Strum the chords in the rhythm indicated. Use the chord diagrams found at the top of the first page of the arrangement for the appropriate chord voicings. The melody and lyrics are also shown to help you keep your spot and sing along.

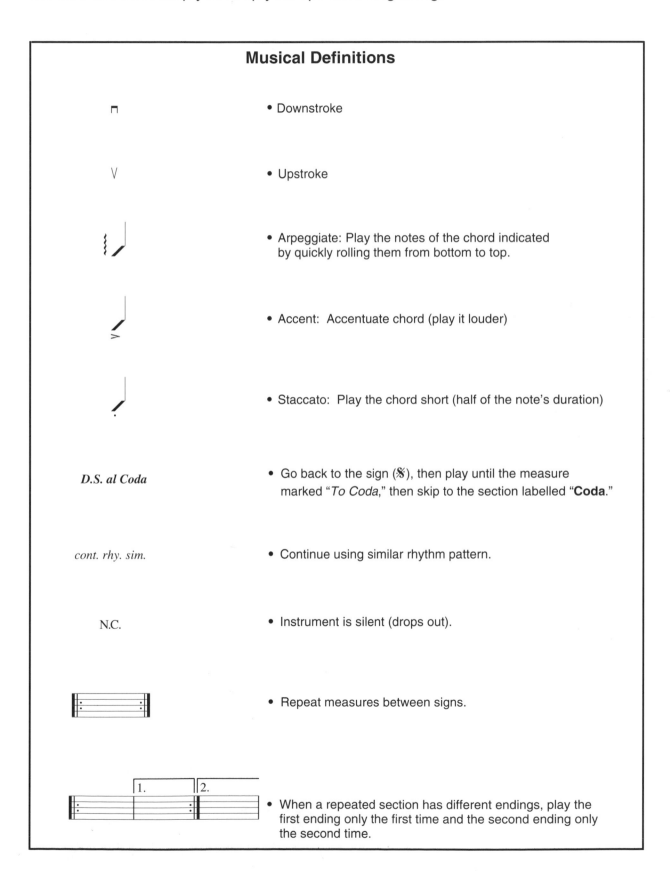

Musical Definitions

- Downstroke

- Upstroke

- Arpeggiate: Play the notes of the chord indicated by quickly rolling them from bottom to top.

- Accent: Accentuate chord (play it louder)

- Staccato: Play the chord short (half of the note's duration)

D.S. al Coda
- Go back to the sign (𝄋), then play until the measure marked "*To Coda*," then skip to the section labelled "**Coda**."

cont. rhy. sim.
- Continue using similar rhythm pattern.

N.C.
- Instrument is silent (drops out).

- Repeat measures between signs.

1.   2.
- When a repeated section has different endings, play the first ending only the first time and the second ending only the second time.

STRUM IT GUITAR

• AUTHENTIC CHORDS • ORIGINAL KEYS • COMPLETE SONGS •

The *Strum It* series lets players strum the chords and sing along with their favorite hits. Each song has been selected because it can be played with regular open chords, barre chords, or other moveable chord types. Guitarists can simply play the rhythm, or play and sing along through the entire song. All songs are shown in their original keys complete with chords, strum patterns, melody and lyrics. Wherever possible, the chord voicings from the recorded versions are notated.

Acoustic Classics
Play along with the recordings of 21 acoustic classics. Songs include: And I Love Her • Angie • Barely Breathing • Free Fallin' • Maggie May • Melissa • Mr. Jones • Only Wanna Be with You • Patience • Signs • Teach Your Children • Wonderful Tonight • Wonderwall • Yesterday • and more. 00699238 $10.95

The Beatles Favorites
Features 23 classic Beatles hits, including: Can't Buy Me Love • Eight Days a Week • Hey Jude • I Saw Her Standing There • Let It Be • Nowhere Man • She Loves You • Something • Yesterday • You've Got to Hide Your Love Away • and more. 00699249 $14.95

Celtic Guitar Songbook
Features 35 complete songs in their original keys, with authentic chords, strum patterns, melody and lyrics. Includes: Black Velvet Band • Cockles and Mussels (Molly Malone) • Danny Boy (Londonderry Air) • Finnegan's Wake • Galway Bay • I'm a Rover and Seldom Sober • The Irish Washerwoman • Kerry Dance • Killarney • McNamara's Band • My Wild Irish Rose • The Rose of Tralee • Sailor's Hornpipe • Whiskey in the Jar • Wild Rover • and more. 00699265 $9.95

Christmas Songs for Guitar
Over 40 Christmas favorites, including: The Christmas Song (Chestnuts Roasting on an Open Fire) • Feliz Navidad • Frosty the Snow Man • Grandma Got Run Over by a Reindeer • The Greatest Gift of All • I'll Be Home for Christmas • It's Beginning to Look Like Christmas • Rockin' Around the Christmas Tree • Silver Bells • and more. 00699247 $9.95

Christmas Songs with Three Chords
30 all-time favorites: Angels We Have Heard on High • Away in a Manger • Deck the Hall • Go, Tell It on the Mountain • Here We Come A-Wassailing • I Heard the Bells on Christmas Day • Jolly Old St. Nicholas • Silent Night • Up on the Housetop • and more. 00699487 $8.95

Country Strummin'
Features 24 songs: Achy Breaky Heart • Adalida • Ain't That Lonely Yet • Blue • The Beaches of Cheyenne • A Broken Wing • Gone Country • I Fall to Pieces • My Next Broken Heart • She and I • Unchained Melody • What a Crying Shame • and more. 00699119 $8.95

Jim Croce - Classic Hits
Authentic chords to 22 great songs from Jim Croce, including: Bad, Bad Leroy Brown • I'll Have to Say I Love You in a Song • Operator (That's Not the Way It Feels) • Time in a Bottle • and more. 00699269 $10.95

Disney Favorites
A great collection of 34 easy-to-play Disney favorites. Includes: Can You Feel the Love Tonight • Circle of Life • Cruella De Vil • Friend Like Me • It's a Small World • Some Day My Prince Will Come • Under the Sea • Whistle While You Work • Winnie the Pooh • Zero to Hero • and more. 00699171 $10.95

Disney Greats
Easy arrangements with guitar chord frames and strum patterns for 39 wonderful Disney classics including: Arabian Nights • The Aristocats • Beauty and the Beast • Colors of the Wind • Go the Distance • Hakuna Matata • Heigh-Ho • Kiss the Girl • A Pirate's Life • When You Wish Upon a Star • Zip-A-Dee-Doo-Dah • Theme from Zorro • and more. 00699172 $10.95

Best of The Doors
Strum along with more than 25 of your favorite hits from The Doors. Includes: Been Down So Long • Hello I Love You Won't You Tell Me Your Name? • Light My Fire • Riders on the Storm • Touch Me • and more. 00699177 $10.95

Favorite Songs with 3 Chords
27 popular songs that are easy to play, including: All Shook Up • Blue Suede Shoes • Boot Scootin' Boogie • Evil Ways • Great Balls of Fire • Lay Down Sally • Semi-Charmed Life • Surfin' U.S.A. • Twist and Shout • Wooly Bully • and more. 00699112 $8.95

Favorite Songs with 4 Chords
22 tunes in this great collection, including: Beast of Burden • Don't Be Cruel • Get Back • Gloria • I Fought the Law • La Bamba • Last Kiss • Let Her Cry • Love Stinks • Peggy Sue • 3 AM • Wild Thing • and more. 00699270 $8.95

Irving Berlin's God Bless America
25 patriotic anthems: Amazing Grace • America, the Beautiful • Battle Hymn of the Republic • From a Distance • God Bless America • Imagine • The Lord's Prayer • The Star Spangled Banner • Stars and Stripes Forever • This Land Is Your Land • United We Stand • You're a Grand Old Flag • and more. 00699508 $9.95

Great '50s Rock
28 of early rock's biggest hits, including: At the Hop • Blueberry Hill • Bye Bye Love • Hound Dog • Rock Around the Clock • That'll Be the Day • and more. 00699187 $8.95

Great '60s Rock
Features the chords, strum patterns, melody and lyrics for 27 classic rock songs, all in their original keys. Includes: And I Love Her • Crying • Gloria • Good Lovin' • I Fought the Law • Mellow Yellow • Return to Sender • Runaway • Surfin' U.S.A. • The Twist • Twist and Shout • Under the Boardwalk • Wild Thing • and more. 00699188 $8.95

Great '70s Rock
Strum the chords to 21 classic '70s hits! Includes: Band on the Run • Burning Love • If • It's a Heartache • Lay Down Sally • Let It Be • Love Hurts • Maggie May • New Kid in Town • Ramblin' Man • Time for Me to Fly • Two Out of Three Ain't Bad • Wild World • and more. 00699262 $8.95

Great '80s Rock
23 arrangements that let you play along with your favorite recordings from the 1980s, such as: Back on the Chain Gang • Centerfold • Free Fallin' • Got My Mind Set on You • Kokomo • Should I Stay or Should I Go • Uptown Girl • Waiting for a Girl Like You • What I Like About You • and more. 00699263 $8.95

Best of Woody Guthrie
20 of the Guthrie's most popular songs, including: Do Re Mi • The Grand Coulee Dam • I Ain't Got No Home • Ramblin' Round • Roll On, Columbia • So Long It's Been Good to Know Yuh (Dusty Old Dust) • Talking Dust Bowl • This Land Is Your Land • Tom Joad • and more. 00699496 $12.95

The John Hiatt Collection
This collection includes 17 classics: Angel Eyes • Feels Like Rain • Have a Little Faith in Me • Memphis in the Meantime • Perfectly Good Guitar • A Real Fine Love • Riding with the King • Thing Called Love (Are You Ready for This Thing Called Love) • The Way We Make a Broken Heart • and more. 00699398 $12.95

Hymn Favorites
Includes: Amazing Grace • Battle Hymn of the Republic • Down by the Riverside • Holy, Holy, Holy • Just as I Am • Rock of Ages • This Is My Father's World • What a Friend We Have in Jesus • and more. 00699271 $9.95

Best of Sarah McLachlan
20 of Sarah's most popular hits for guitar, including: Adia • Angel • Building a Mystery • I Will Remember You • Ice Cream • Sweet Surrender • and more. 00699231 $10.95

A Merry Christmas Songbook
Easy arrangements for 51 holiday hits: Away in a Manger • Deck the Hall • Fum, Fum, Fum • The Holly and the Ivy • Jolly Old St. Nicholas • O Christmas Tree • Star of the East • The Twelve Days of Christmas • and more! 00699211 $8.95

Pop-Rock Guitar Favorites
31 songs, including: Angie • Brown Eyed Girl • Crazy Little Thing Called Love • Eight Days a Week • Fire and Rain • Free Bird • Gloria • Hey Jude • Let It Be • Maggie May • New Kid in Town • Surfin' U.S.A. • Wild Thing • Wonderful Tonight • and more. 00699088 $8.95

Best of George Strait
Strum the chords to 20 great Strait hits! Includes: Adalida • All My Ex's Live in Texas • The Best Day • Blue Clear Sky • Carried Away • The Chair • Does Fort Worth Ever Cross Your Mind • Lovebug • Right or Wrong • Write This Down • and more. 00699235 $10.95

Best of Hank Williams Jr.
24 of Hank's signature standards. Includes: Ain't Misbehavin' • All My Rowdy Friends Are Coming Over Tonight • Attitude Adjustment • Family Tradition • Honky Tonkin' • Texas Women • There's a Tear in My Beer • Whiskey Bent and Hell Bound • and more. 00699224 $10.95

Women of Rock
22 hits from today's top female artists. Includes: Bitch • Don't Speak • Galileo • Give Me One Reason • I Don't Want to Wait • Insensitive • Lovefool • Mother Mother • Stay • Torn • You Oughta Know • You Were Meant for Me • Zombie • and more. 00699183 $9.95

FOR MORE INFORMATION, SEE YOUR LOCAL MUSIC DEALER, OR WRITE TO:

HAL•LEONARD®
CORPORATION

7777 W. BLUEMOUND RD. P.O. BOX 13819 MILWAUKEE, WI 53213

www.halleonard.com

0102

GUITAR PLAY-ALONG

The Guitar Play-Along Series will help you play your favorite songs quickly and easily. Just follow the tab and listen to the CD to hear how the guitar should sound, and then play along using the separate backing tracks. Mac or PC users can also slow down the tempo by using the CD in their computer. The melody and lyrics are also included in the book in case you want to sing, or to simply help you follow along. 8 songs in each book.

VOLUME 1 – ROCK GUITAR
Day Tripper • Message in a Bottle • Refugee • Shattered • Sunshine of Your Love • Takin' Care of Business • Tush • Walk This Way.
00699570 Book/CD Pack........................$12.95

VOLUME 2 – ACOUSTIC GUITAR
Angie • Behind Blue Eyes • Best of My Love • Blackbird • Dust in the Wind • Layla • Night Moves • Yesterday.
00699569 Book/CD Pack........................$12.95

VOLUME 3 – HARD ROCK
Crazy Train • Iron Man • Living After Midnight • Rock You like a Hurricane • Round and Round • Smoke on the Water • Sweet Child O' Mine • You Really Got Me.
00699573 Book/CD Pack........................$14.95

VOLUME 4 – POP/ROCK
Breakdown • Crazy Little Thing Called Love • Hit Me with Your Best Shot • I Want You to Want Me • Lights • R.O.C.K. in the U.S.A. (A Salute to 60's Rock) • Summer of '69 • What I like About You.
_____00699571 Book/CD Pack........................$12.95

VOLUME 5 – MODERN ROCK
Aerials • Alive • Bother • Chop Suey! • Control • Last Resort • Take a Look Around (Theme from "M:I-2") • Wish You Were Here.
_____00699574 Book/CD Pack........................$12.95

VOLUME 6 – '90S ROCK
Are You Gonna Go My Way • Come Out and Play • I'll Stick Around • Know Your Enemy • Man in the Box • Outshined • Smells like Teen Spirit • Under the Bridge.
_____00699572 Book/CD Pack........................$12.95

VOLUME 7 – BLUES GUITAR
All Your Love (I Miss Loving) • Born Under a Bad Sign • Crosscut Saw • I'm Tore Down • Pride and Joy • The Sky Is Crying • Sweet Home Chicago • The Thrill Is Gone.
_____00699575 Book/CD Pack........................$12.95

VOLUME 8 – ROCK
All Right Now • Black Magic Woman • Get Back • Hey Joe • Layla • Love Me Two Times • Won't Get Fooled Again • You Really Got Me.
_____00699585 Book/CD Pack........................$12.95

VOLUME 9 – PUNK ROCK
All the Small Things • Fat Lip • Flavor of the Weak • Hash Pipe • I Feel So • Pretty Fly (For a White Guy) • Say It Ain't So • Self Esteem.
_____00699576 Book/CD Pack........................$12.95

VOLUME 10 – ACOUSTIC
Have You Ever Really Loved a Woman? • Here Comes the Sun • The Magic Bus • Norwegian Wood (This Bird Has Flown) • Space Oddity • Spanish Caravan • Tangled up in Blue • Tears in Heaven.
_____00699586 Book/CD Pack........................$12.95

VOLUME 11 – EARLY ROCK
Fun, Fun, Fun • Hound Dog • Louie, Louie • No Particular Place to Go • Oh, Pretty Woman • Rock Around the Clock • Under the Boardwalk • Wild Thing.
_____00699579 Book/CD Pack........................$12.95

VOLUME 12 – POP/ROCK
Every Breath You Take • I Wish It Would Rain • Money for Nothing • Rebel, Rebel • Run to You • Ticket to Ride • Wonderful Tonight • You Give Love a Bad Name.
_____00699587 Book/CD Pack........................$12.95

VOLUME 13 – FOLK ROCK
Leaving on a Jet Plane • Suite: Judy Blue Eyes • Take Me Home, Country Roads • This Land Is   Your Land • Time in a Bottle • Turn! Turn! Turn! (To Everything There Is a Season) • You've Got a Friend • You've Got to Hide Your Love Away.
_____00699581 Book/CD Pack........................$12.95

VOLUME 14 – BLUES ROCK
Blue on Black • Crossfire • Cross Road Blues (Crossroads) • The House Is Rockin' • La Grange • Move It on Over • Roadhouse Blues • Statesboro Blues.
_____00699582 Book/CD Pack........................$12.95

VOLUME 15 – R&B
Ain't Too Proud to Beg • Brick House • Get Ready • I Can't Help Myself (Sugar Pie, Honey Bunch) • I Got You (I Feel Good) • I Heard It Through the Grapevine • My Girl • Shining Star.
_____00699583 Book/CD Pack........................$12.95

VOLUME 16 – JAZZ
All Blues • Black Orpheus • Bluesette • Footprints • Misty • Satin Doll • Stella by Starlight • Tenor Madness.
_____00699584 Book/CD Pack........................$12.95

VOLUME 17 – COUNTRY
All My Rowdy Friends Are Coming over Tonight • Amie • Boot Scootin' Boogie • Chattahoochee • Folsom Prison Blues • Friends in Low Places • T-R-O-U-B-L-E • Workin' Man Blues.
_____00699588 Book/CD Pack........................$12.95

VOLUME 18 – ACOUSTIC ROCK
About a Girl • Breaking the Girl • Drive • Iris • More Than Words • Patience • Silent Lucidity • 3 AM.
_____00699577 Book/CD Pack........................$12.95

VOLUME 19 – SOUL
Get up (I Feel like Being) a Sex Machine • Green Onions • In the Midnight Hour • Knock on Wood • Mustang Sally • (Sittin' On) the Dock of the Bay • Soul Man • Walkin' the Dog.
_____00699578 Book/CD Pack........................$12.95

VOLUME 20 – ROCKABILLY
Blue Suede Shoes • Bluejean Bop • Hello Mary Lou • Little Sister • Mystery Train • Rock This Town • Stray Cat Strut • That'll Be the Day.
_____00699580 Book/CD Pack........................$12.95

Prices, contents, and availability subject to change without notice.

FOR MORE INFORMATION, SEE YOUR LOCAL MUSIC DEALER, OR WRITE TO:

HAL•LEONARD
CORPORATION
7777 W. BLUEMOUND RD. P.O. BOX 13819 MILWAUKEE, WI 53213

Visit Hal Leonard online at www.halleonard.com

MASTER THE *Blues*

The Songs and Licks That Made It Happen
by Fred Sokolow
A complete survey of a musical genre, its pioneers and how it developed, including: Six note-for-note transcriptions of famous tunes pivotal to the genre; extensive instruction in the essential playing styles of the genre, using scales, chords, licks, and musical exercises; the history of the development of each playing style; biographies of the pioneering artists; a recording of the songs, exercises, and licks.

With guitar instruction from Hal Leonard
All books include notes and tab.

Inside the Blues 1942-1982
by Dave Rubin
The definitive blues collection! Over 150 pages spanning 40 years of blues history with techniques of the greatest blues guitarists of all time, including T-Bone Walker, Muddy Waters, Elmore James, B.B. King, Otis Rush, Buddy Guy, Albert King, Jimi Hendrix, Johnny Winter, Stevie Ray Vaughan, and many more. Includes instruction and musical examples – an essential volume for any student of the blues!
00696558 ....$24.95

Art of the Shuffle
by Dave Rubin
This method book explores shuffle, boogie and swing rhythms for guitar. Includes tab and notation, and covers Delta, country, Chicago, Kansas City, Texas, New Orleans, West Coast, and bebop blues. Also includes audio for demonstration of each style and to jam along with.
00695005 Book/CD Pack $19.95

Power Trio Blues
by Dave Rubin
This book/CD pack details how to play electric guitar in a trio with bass and drums. Boogie, shuffle, and slow blues rhythms, licks, double stops, chords, and bass patterns are presented for full and exciting blues. A CD with the music examples performed by a smokin' power trio is included for play-along instruction and jamming.
00695028 Book/CD Pack $19.95

Basic Blues for Guitar
The most thorough blues guitar book yet. Over 35 blues tunes covering electric and rock blues, folk, fingerpicking and bottleneck blues, B.B. King and Chuck Berry styles, jazzy blues and more. Plus positions, scales chords, discographies and an overview of styles from Robert Johnson to George Benson. Written in music tablature with chord grids. All tunes are played on the stereo cassette that comes with the book.
00699002 Bk/Cassette Pack................$16.95

Lead Blues Licks
by Michael P. Wolfsohn
This book examines blues licks in the styles of such greats as B.B. King, Albert King, Stevie Ray Vaughan, Eric Clapton, Chuck Berry, and more. You'll progress from the standard blues progression and blues scale to the various techniques of bending, fast pull offs and hammer-ons, double stops, and more.
00699325..$6.95

Acoustic Country Blues
Delta Blues Before Robert Johnson
Inside the Blues
by Dave Rubin
A valuable collection of 12 classic song transcriptions complete with detailed instruction and photos. The songs include: Cross Road Blues (Crossroads) • I Believe I'll Dust My Broom • I'm Gonna Yola My Blues Away • Lead Pencil Blues • Life Saver Blues • Roll and Tumble Blues • You Gonna Need Somebody When You Die • and more.
00695139 Book/CD Pack $16.95

Birth of the Groove
R&B, Soul and Funk Guitar: 1940-1965
by Dave Rubin
The years 1945-1965 saw a radical and exciting shift in American popular music. Blues and swing jazz helped to produce a new musical form called rhythm and blues, which in turn set in motion the development of soul and funk, not to mention rock 'n' roll. This book/CD pack explores everything from the swinging boogie of Tiny Grimes to the sweaty primal funk of Jimmy Nolen, and everyone in between. The CD includes 45 full-band tracks.
00695036 Book/CD Pack $17.95

Electric Slide Guitar
by David Hamburger
This book/audio method explores the basic fundamentals of slide guitar: from selecting a slide and proper setup of the guitar, to open and standard tuning. Plenty of music examples are presented showing sample licks as well as backup/rhythm slide work. Each section also examines techniques and solos in the style of the best slide guitarists, including Duane Allman, Dave Hole, Ry Cooder, Bonnie Raitt, Muddy Waters, Johnny Winter and Elmore James.
00695022 Book/CD Pack $19.95

101 Must-Know Blues Licks
A Quick, Easy Reference for All Guitarists
by Wolf Marshall
Now you can add authentic blues feel and flavor to your playing! Here are 101 definitive licks – plus a demonstration CD – from every major blues guitar style, neatly organized into easy-to-use categories. They're all here, including Delta blues, jump blues, country blues, Memphis blues, Texas blues, West Coast blues, Chicago blues, and British blues.
00695318 Book/CD Pack $16.95

Fretboard Roadmaps Blues Guitar
for Acoustic and Electric Guitar
by Fred Sokolow
These essential fretboard patterns are roadmaps that all great blues guitarists know and use. This book teaches how to: play lead and rhythm anywhere on the fretboard, in any key; play a variety of lead guitar styles; play chords and progressions anywhere on the fretboard, in any key; expand chord vocabulary; learn to think musicially, the way the pros do.
00695350 Book/CD Pack $14.95

12-Bar Blues
by Dave Rubin
The term "12-bar blues" has become synonymous with blues music and is the basis for an incredible body of jazz, rock 'n' roll, and other forms of popular music. This book/CD pack is solely devoted to providing guitarists with all the technical tools necessary for playing 12-bar blues with authority. The CD includes 24 full-band tracks. Covers: boogie, shuffle, swing, riff, and jazzy blues progressions; Chicago, minor, slow, bebop, and other blues styles; soloing, intros, turnarounds, and more.
00695187 Book/CD Pack $16.95

The Roots of Acoustic Blues
Songs include: Baby, Please Don't Go • Come Back Baby • Diddy Wah Diddy • Hey Hey • I'm So Glad.

00699068 Book/CD Pack $16.95

The Roots of Electric Blues
Songs include: The Things I Used to Do • Hideaway • Killing Floor • Mean Old World • I Can't Quit You Baby • Why I Sing the Blues.

00699067 Book/CD Pack $16.95

The Roots of Slide Guitar
Songs include: Come On in My Kitchen • Motherless Children • Roll and Tumble Blues • You Can't Lose What You Ain't Never Had • You Gotta Move • You Shook Me.
00699083 Book/CD Pack $16.95

Blues You Can Use
by John Ganapes
A comprehensive source for learning blues guitar, designed to develop both your lead and rhythm playing. Covers all styles of blues, including Texas, Delta, R&B, early rock and roll, gospel, blues/rock and more. Includes 21 complete solos; extensive instruction; audio with leads and full band backing; and more!
00695007 Book/CD Pack..............................$19.95

Blues You Can Use Book of Guitar Chords
by John Ganapes
A reference guide to blues, R&B, jazz, and rock rhythm guitar, with hundreds of voicings, chord theory construction, chord progressions and exercises and much more. The Blues You Can Use Book Of Guitar Chords is useful for the beginner to advanced player.
00695082...$14.95

More Blues You Can Use
by John Ganapes
A complete guide to learning blues guitar, covering scales, rhythms, chords, patterns, rakes, techniques, and more. CD includes 13 full-demo solos.
00695165 Book/CD Pack $19.95

Blues Licks You Can Use
by John Ganapes
Contains music and performance notes for 75 hot lead phrases, covering styles including up-tempo and slow blues, jazz-blues, shuffle blues, swing blues and more! CD features full-band examples.
00695386 Book/CD Pack $16.95

FOR MORE INFORMATION, SEE YOUR LOCAL MUSIC DEALER,
OR WRITE TO:

HAL•LEONARD®
CORPORATION
7777 W. BLUEMOUND RD. P.O. BOX 13819 MILWAUKEE, WI 53213

Prices, availability, and contents subject to change without notice. Some products may not be available outside the U.S.A.

0303